discovermore

Good Health

Minerals

Ursula Pang

Britannica
Educational Publishing
IN ASSOCIATION WITH
THE ROSEN PUBLISHING GROUP

Published in 2027 by Britannica Educational Publishing (a trademark of Encyclopædia Britannica, Inc.) in association with The Rosen Publishing Group, Inc.
2544 Clinton Street, Buffalo, NY 14224

Distributed exclusively by Rosen Publishing.
To see additional Britannica Educational Publishing titles, go to rosenpublishing.com.

Editor: Greg Roza
Book Design: Michael Flynn

Photo Credits: Cover Mykolal Mykolal/Shutterstock.com; (series background) Dai Yim/Shutterstock.com; p. 4 malshkoff/Shutterstock.com; p. 5 Tatevosian Yana/Shutterstock.com; p. 6 Dream79/Shutterstock.com; p. 7 Jr images/Shutterstock.com; p. 9 (top) Kyle Oster/Shutterstock.com; p. 9 (bottom) Ekaterina_Minaeva/Shutterstock.com; p. 10 Designua/Shutterstock.com; pp. 11, 13 (top) monticello/Shutterstock.com; p. 13 (bottom) stockcreations/Shutterstock.com; p. 14 Halfpoint/Shutterstock.com; p. 15 Brent Hofacker/Shutterstock.com; p. 16 Dee-sign/Shutterstock.com; p. 17 gowithstock/Shutterstock.com; p. 18 T.Vyc/Shutterstock.com; p. 19 Tatjana Baibakova/Shutterstock.com; p. 20 DenisMArt/Shutterstock.com; p. 21 gaometri/Shutterstock.com; p. 22 Billy F Blume Jr/Shutterstock.com; p. 23 Foxys Forest Manufacture/Shutterstock.com; p. 24 fast-stock/Shutterstock.com; p. 25 rom_olik/Shutterstock.com; p. 26 Robert Kneschke/Shutterstock.com; p. 27 Yuliia Ushakova/Shutterstock.com; p. 28 Satria_Photo/Shutterstock.com; p. 29 Red Fox studio/Shutterstock.com.

Cataloging-in-Publication Data

Names: Pang, Ursula.
Title: Minerals / Ursula Pang.
Description: Buffalo, New York : Britannica Educational Publishing, an imprint of Rosen Publishing, 2027. | Series: Discover more: good health | Includes glossary and index.
Identifiers: ISBN 9781641905923 (pbk.) | ISBN 9781641905930 (library bound) | ISBN 9781641905947 (ebook)
Subjects: LCSH: Minerals in nutrition--Juvenile literature. | Food--Mineral content--Juvenile literature.
Classification: LCC QP533.P36 2027 | DDC 613.285--dc23

Manufactured in the United States of America

CPSIA Compliance Information: Batch #CSBRIT27. For further information contact Rosen Publishing at 1-800-237-9932.

Contents

Meet the Minerals

Nutrients are things that a body needs in order to grow and stay healthy. They are an important part of the human diet. Minerals are a kind of nutrient. Certain daily amounts of dietary minerals are required for strong bones, muscles, and other parts of the body.

Minerals are inorganic substances, meaning that they come from rocks and other nonliving things. Plants take in minerals from the soil. Animals obtain minerals by eating plants and the milk, eggs, and meat of plant-eating animals.

Plants take in minerals from the soil through their roots. They use minerals and other nutrients to grow and thrive.

People need minerals too! We get minerals from the foods we eat. Blueberries are a good source of calcium, potassium, and other essential minerals.

Nutritionists are experts who give advice on how food affects health. They sort minerals into two categories: macrominerals and trace minerals.

Macrominerals are also called major minerals. People need to consume more than 100 milligrams, or 3.5 ounces, of these minerals every day. Calcium, magnesium, phosphorus, sulfur, sodium, potassium, and chloride are macrominerals.

People need smaller amounts of each trace mineral—less than 100 milligrams daily. The trace minerals include iron, zinc, copper, manganese, iodine, selenium, fluoride, molybdenum, and chromium.

Consider This

Why is it important to get enough minerals in your diet when you are young and your body is growing?

Minerals and the Human Body

Most nutrients provide energy for the body's activities. They are **metabolized** by the body. Minerals, on the other hand, are not metabolized. They do not provide energy.

Minerals perform different functions. They provide structure—for example, calcium makes bones hard. They also do specific jobs—for example, iron helps blood to carry oxygen around the body. Some minerals are particles with an electric charge. They help to regulate processes in the body.

Dairy products such as these are high in calcium.

Nuts such as almonds, peanuts, and cashews are excellent sources of magnesium.

Minerals make up about 4 to 6 percent of a person's body weight. About one half of this amount is calcium. About one quarter is phosphorus, which is also found in bones and teeth. Trace minerals do not add much to body weight.

Most minerals are involved in a variety of functions. For instance, magnesium helps the muscles work. It also helps to build bones and to control blood sugar levels.

WORD WISE

WHEN NUTRIENTS ARE METABOLIZED, THE BODY BREAKS THEM DOWN TO USE FOR ENERGY AND TO GROW AND HEAL. THE PROCESS OF METABOLIZING IS CALLED METABOLISM.

Amounts of minerals in a food can vary depending on the type of food it is. A plant's mineral content, for example, can depend on growing conditions. Cooking methods can reduce the minerals in food. Some foods, such as salt and cereal, have minerals added to them to make them more nutritious. These are called fortified foods.

The body must absorb dietary minerals to use them. Various factors affect how well the body absorbs minerals. In general, minerals are better absorbed from animal foods than from plant foods. Also, minerals can interact with each other. This means that the presence of one mineral can decrease the absorption of another. A person's physical condition can affect absorption as well.

Most packaged foods have labels that show nutritional information, including amounts of minerals. These amounts include minerals that are naturally in the food and minerals that were added through fortification. Nutrition labels help consumers make healthy choices about minerals.

Table salt is often fortified with the mineral iodine. Our bodies need iodine for several processes that are essential for overall health.

compare and contrast

Check the food labels of some of your favorite foods. What minerals do they contain?

Nutrition fact labels help people to choose the healthiest options when shopping.

Healthy Bones and Teeth

People need calcium at every stage of their lives. Kids need calcium to build strong bones and teeth. Adults need calcium to prevent bones from becoming weak. People who do not get enough calcium are at a high risk of having **osteoporosis** later in life.

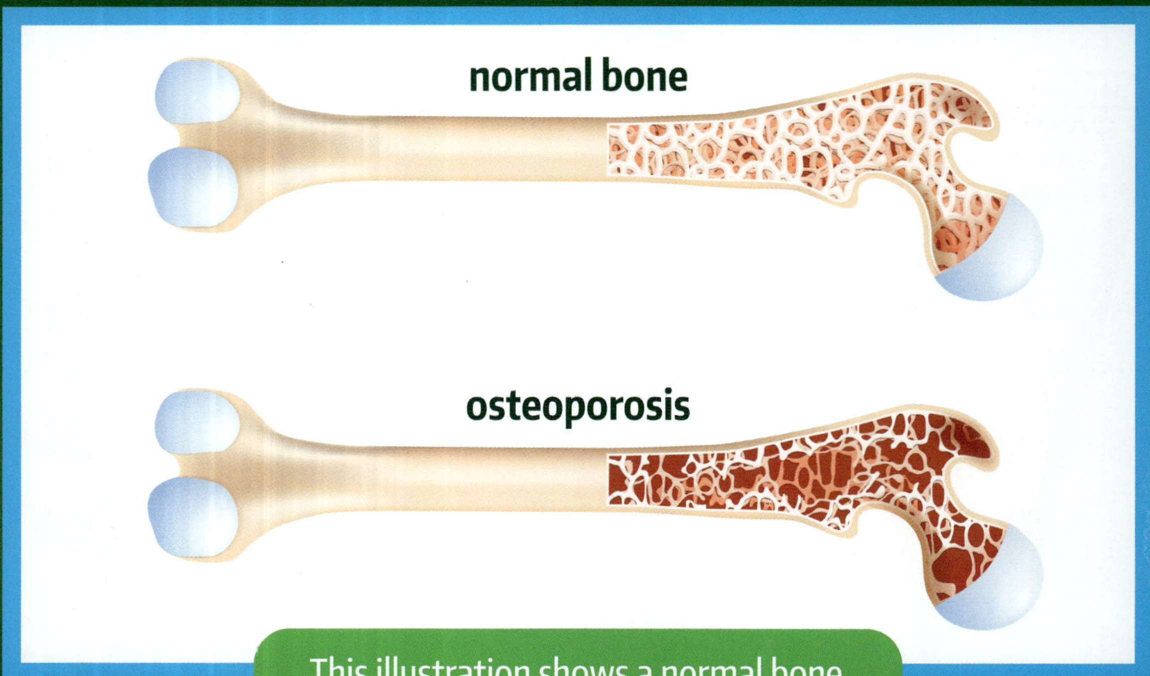

This illustration shows a normal bone compared to a bone with osteoporosis.

Dairy products are high in calcium, but many other foods contain it too.

Calcium performs other important functions in the body, too. It helps muscles to contract, or tighten, when they move. It also plays a role in sending messages through the nervous system.

Many people, especially tweens and teenagers, do not get enough calcium in their diet. Milk and dairy products are great sources of calcium. Other foods high in calcium include fish (especially fish like sardines, where the bones are eaten) and green leafy vegetables. Some foods, such as orange juice and cereal, are fortified with calcium.

WORD WISE

OSTEOPOROSIS IS A DISEASE IN WHICH BONES BECOME THIN AND BRITTLE AND CAN BREAK EASILY.

Magnesium, Phosphorus, and Sulfur

Magnesium is an important mineral in regulating many processes in the body. Some of these include muscle and nerve function, regulation of blood sugar levels, and the heartbeat. Magnesium also helps to build bones and to produce protein and energy. Good sources of magnesium include green leafy vegetables, legumes (including beans, peas, and lentils), nuts, and whole grains.

Phosphorus is needed to build bones and teeth. It is also involved in other functions, such as the growth and repair of cells in the body.

The mineral sulfur is part of some of the building blocks that make up cells. It also plays a role in cellular respiration, which is the process that cells go through to get energy from nutrients.

Phosphorus and sulfur are found in many foods. Most people do not have to seek out specific foods containing these minerals. Sunflower seeds, Romano cheese, and salmon contain phosphorus. Cauliflower and other members of the cabbage family are rich in sulfur.

Some common sources of magnesium include almonds, spinach, beans, bananas, and avocados.

compare and contrast

Magnesium is found in chlorophyll, the substance that makes plants green. Many plant foods are good sources of magnesium. Sulfur is found in protein, which makes up muscles. Can you name foods you eat that probably contain sulfur?

Eggs are a good source of sulfur, but cauliflower and cabbage are also healthy sources of the mineral.

Here Come the Electrolytes

Electrolytes are substances that control the movement of fluids in and out of cells, including the blood. Drinking plenty of water is important in order to keep a balance of electrolytes and to avoid dehydration. The minerals sodium, potassium, and chloride act as electrolytes in the body.

Sports drinks often have electrolytes added to them to help active people maintain a fluid balance in their body.

Bananas are rich in potassium.

Each of these minerals has other important functions, too. For example, sodium and potassium play roles in the function of muscle and nerve cells. Chloride, found in stomach acid, aids in digestion.

Potassium is found in meat, poultry, some fish, certain vegetables (especially sweet potatoes and squash), certain fruits (especially bananas), nuts, and dairy products. Sodium and chloride make up table salt. Most people do not have to worry about getting the required amount of these minerals.

WORD WISE

ELECTROLYTES ARE IONS, OR PARTICLES WITH AN ELECTRIC CHARGE. THEY HELP TO REGULATE PROCESSES PERFORMED BY THE CELLS OF THE BODY.

Trace Minerals

Trace minerals are those that people require in much smaller amounts than macrominerals. Iron is a trace mineral that's very important to our health. Most iron in the body is contained in red blood cells. The body uses iron to build a substance called hemoglobin in the blood. Hemoglobin carries oxygen to all the cells in the body. Oxygen and hemoglobin combine to give blood its red color. The body's cells use the oxygen to do their jobs. Iron is also responsible for other functions, such as supporting metabolism and keeping cells healthy.

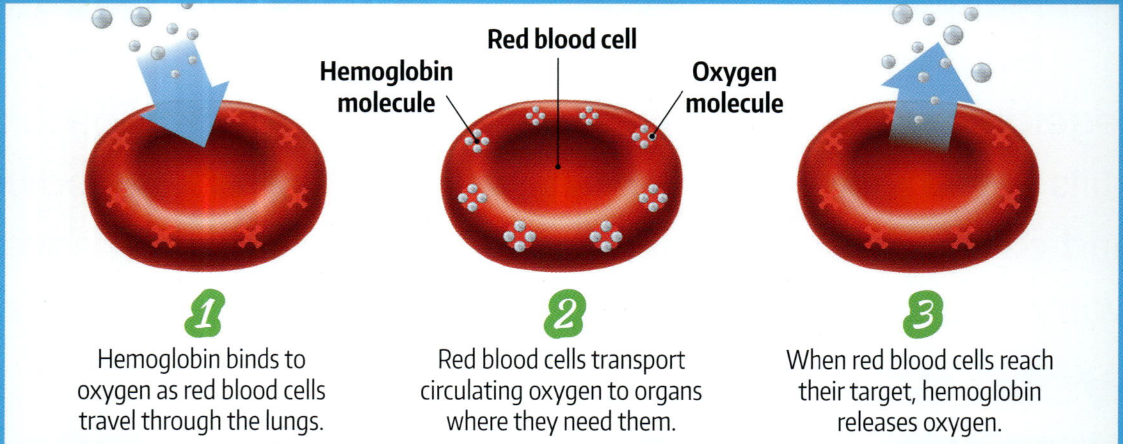

We need iron to maintain a healthy level of hemoglobin in our body.

Chicken liver is high in iron. Pairing liver with lime juice (vitamin C) helps the body absorb all the iron it needs to function.

There are two forms of dietary iron. Heme iron is more easily used by the body. It is found in meat, poultry, and seafood. Non-heme iron is found in plants. Sources of non-heme iron include nuts, legumes such as lentils and beans, dried fruits, grains, and vegetables. Vitamin C helps the body absorb iron.

Consider This

Vegetarians do not eat meat or poultry. Why should they take special care to include enough iron in their diets?

Zinc, copper, iodine, manganese, selenium, molybdenum, and chromium are all trace minerals. They may not sounds as familiar as calcium or potassium, but they are all important in keeping the body healthy.

The mineral zinc is the second most plentiful trace mineral in the body, behind iron. It plays an important role in the **immune system** and in the senses of smell and taste. Children need zinc for healthy growth and development. Good sources of zinc include oysters, meat (such as lamb and beef), poultry, beans, and nuts.

Most seafood is high in zinc, but oysters have the highest content of the mineral.

Shellfish is low in fat and highly nutritious. It contains protein as well as several key vitamins and minerals, including zinc and copper.

Iodine is important for the function of an organ called the thyroid gland. The thyroid gland uses iodine to produce a substance called thyroxine. Thyroxine helps the body's cells to function normally. Iodine occurs in plants and animals from the sea, such as shellfish and seaweed. Dairy products also contain iodine. Table salt often is fortified with iodine as well.

Copper helps to produce red blood cells. It also supports nerve cells and the immune system. Copper is found in oysters and other shellfish, whole grains, liver, and dark leafy green vegetables.

WORD WISE

THE IMMUNE SYSTEM PROTECTS THE BODY FROM GERMS AND OTHER OUTSIDE SUBSTANCES THAT CAN CAUSE DISEASE.

The trace mineral manganese plays a role in the action of many enzymes, which are proteins that perform specific jobs. Manganese also is important in the reproductive system. Dietary sources of manganese include nuts, seeds, whole grains, legumes, green leafy vegetables, and tea.

Dietary manganese is found in many foods. Seeds and nuts are great sources for this mineral.

Fluoride is sometimes considered a dietary trace mineral, but it is not required for health. Fluoride is added to toothpaste and water supplies to help prevent tooth decay. Black and green teas are high in natural fluoride.

Selenium helps the body to make enzymes. Some of these enzymes protect cells from being damaged. Food sources include Brazil nuts, seafood (especially tuna, halibut, and sardines), ham, beef liver, whole grains, and dairy products.

Other trace minerals in the body include molybdenum and chromium. They are present in small amounts. Molybdenum helps certain enzymes to do their jobs. Chromium helps to regulate blood sugar. Some food sources for molybdenum are legumes, grains, and nuts. Chromium is found in broccoli and grape juice.

Consider This

Have you noticed that green leafy vegetables contain many important minerals? What is your favorite way to eat your greens?

Mineral Deficit

A deficit, or a lack, of minerals over a long period of time can result in disorders. The disorders depend on which mineral is deficient, or missing from the diet. For example, a deficiency of calcium can lead to osteoporosis, especially in older adults.

Nutrition facts labels show the percent daily value (%DV) for each mineral. The percentage shows how much a nutrient in a serving of a food contributes to a recommended dietary allowance.

A vegetarian meal can provide plenty of minerals if it includes a variety of nutritious whole grains, fruits, and vegetables.

How do people know whether they are getting enough minerals? A value called the recommended dietary allowance (RDA) is the daily amount of a nutrient that a person needs. This value is not the same for everyone. It depends on factors such as gender and age. Food labels list the average RDA for every mineral that is included in a serving (based on a daily diet of 2,000 calories).

Consider This

A cup of whole milk has a %DV of about 40 percent. That's close to half of the recommended daily allowance of calcium in 2,000 calorie diet. What other minerals are found in whole milk?

People who restrict their diets, such as vegetarians, may have trouble getting enough dietary minerals. (Vegetarians can get the minerals they need by choosing the right variety of foods.) Some medical conditions can affect digestion or cause a patient to require more minerals. Children, pregnant women, and older adults may be at a higher risk of mineral deficiency.

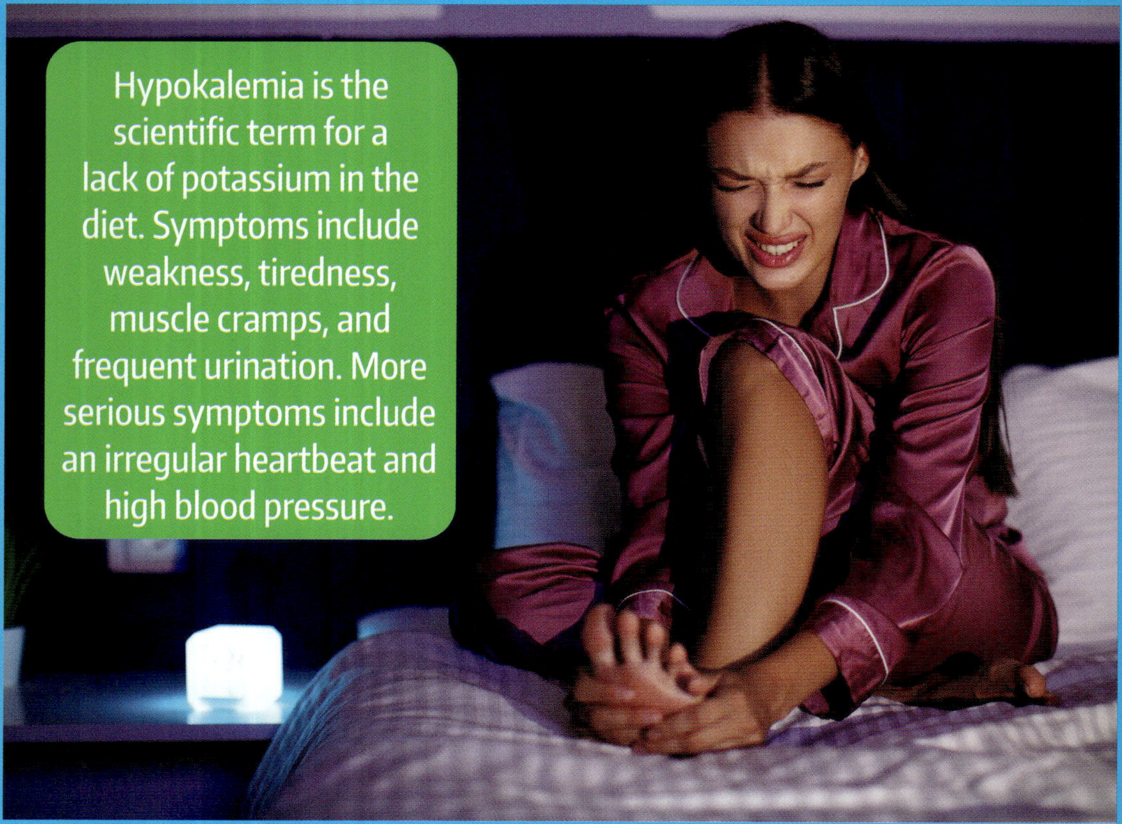

Hypokalemia is the scientific term for a lack of potassium in the diet. Symptoms include weakness, tiredness, muscle cramps, and frequent urination. More serious symptoms include an irregular heartbeat and high blood pressure.

Yogurt mixed with fresh fruit is a great way to get a range of minerals. Whole milk yogurt is a great source of calcium. Raspberries contain significant amounts of potassium, magnesium, phosphorous, and calcium, but they also contain sodium, iron, manganese, copper, and zinc.

The most common mineral deficiency is a lack of iron, which can cause **anemia**. For children, iron deficiency can harm growth, development, and learning ability. An iodine deficiency can cause a condition called goiter. This is a swelling of the thyroid gland in the neck.

It is possible for people to develop deficiencies in zinc, magnesium, or other dietary minerals, but these cases are uncommon. Still, it is a good idea to eat a balanced diet that includes a variety of healthy foods. An overall nutritious diet contains the right levels of minerals for most people. Trying new foods and new food combinations will help you get your daily intake of minerals and other nutrients.

WORD WISE

ANEMIA IS A CONDITION IN WHICH THE BLOOD HAS LESS THAN THE NORMAL AMOUNT OF RED BLOOD CELLS OR HEMOGLOBIN. SYMPTOMS INCLUDE WEAKNESS, EXHAUSTION, PALE SKIN, SHORTNESS OF BREATH, AND ABNORMAL HEARTBEAT.

Mineral Supplements

Although a healthy diet usually provides all the minerals we need, some people take mineral supplements to make sure that they get enough of them. Supplements can contain a single mineral or several minerals. Supplements made up of many minerals and vitamins are called multivitamins. Supplements can treat or prevent mineral deficiencies. Still, it is better to get minerals from whole foods, when possible, because they include other healthful nutrients. Supplements cannot replace a balanced diet.

People who eat plenty of fresh fruits and vegetables usually don't need to take mineral supplements.

Mineral supplements come in different shapes and forms.

In general, parents should check with a doctor before giving supplements to their children. There may be medical issues to consider. For example, supplements can interact with prescription medications.

The government regulates supplements as foods, not as drugs. But supplements are regulated differently than regular foods. Anyone taking a supplement should choose a trusted source. Groups like U.S. Pharmacopeia (USP) set quality standards for supplement makers. Many supplements have side effects. If you feel sick while using a supplement it's important to stop using it right away.

Consider This

If you take a multivitamin, it is probably a children's vitamin. Why should kids not take vitamins for adults?

Too Many Minerals

Some minerals have a value called the tolerable upper intake level (UL). Doses above this amount can make a person very sick. Most people know that too much sodium can cause health problems. These problems can be life-threatening, such as heart disease and stroke. Large doses of other minerals can be harmful as well.

It is easy to get too much sodium in your daily diet. Fast foods and packaged foods often contain more than the recommended daily amount of sodium.

Kids need less iron than adults. Children's multivitamins with iron are packaged to contain safe mineral dosages.

For children, especially, it can be possible to overdose on trace minerals. The RDA value for these minerals is very small. For example, iron can be deadly if a child swallows too many iron supplement pills meant for adults. People who consume a lot of fortified foods or take dietary supplements should make sure that their total amounts of minerals do not exceed safe levels. As always, eating a balanced diet will make sure you're not getting too much of any one mineral.

Consider This

Salt contains the important minerals sodium and chloride, but experts recommend that people restrict salt in their diet. Why could it be bad to use too much salt?

Glossary

absorb To take in or swallow up.
adequate Enough for a requirement.
cell One of the tiny units that are the basic building blocks of living things.
condition A state of being, or a state in which something is wrong.
consume To eat or drink.
content An amount that is contained.
dehydration The loss of water or body fluid.
diet The food and drink that a person, animal, or group takes in.
digestion The conversion of food into simpler forms that can be used by the body.
disorder An abnormal physical or mental condition.
energy Power or ability to be active.
fortified Enriched, or having something useful added.
function The natural action of a part in a living thing.
method A way of doing something.
muscle A body tissue that can contract and produce movement.
organ A part of a person, plant, or animal that consists of cells and tissues and is specialized to do a particular task.
overdose To take too much of something (such as a drug, medicine, or vitamin).
process A continuing action or series of actions; or, to change something from one form into another by preparing or treating it in a special way.
regulate To govern or control.
restrict To place under limits as to use.
structure The arrangement or relationship of parts in a substance, body, or system.

For More Information

Books

Kuehl, Ashley. *Nutrition*. Bloomington MN: SilverTip Books, 2025.

Slingerland, Janet. *Minerals*. St. Paul, MN: North Star Editions, 2024.

Websites

How to Make Healthy Food Choices
kidshealth.org/en/kids/pyramid.html
Read all about nutrition and find links to similarly related topics.

How to Understand and Use the Nutrition Facts Label
www.fda.gov/food/nutrition-facts-label/how-understand-and-use-nutrition-facts-label
Read more about food labels and how to use them at this detailed website from the FDA.

Index